Order this book online at www.trafford.com/07-0014
or email orders@trafford.com

Most Trafford titles are also available at major online book retailers.

Note for Librarians: A cataloguing record for this book is available from Library
and Archives Canada at www.collectionscanada.ca/amicus/index-e.html

Printed in Victoria, BC, Canada.

ISBN: 978-1-4251-1561-6

*We at Trafford believe that it is the responsibility of us all, as both individuals
and corporations, to make choices that are environmentally and socially sound.
You, in turn, are supporting this responsible conduct each time you purchase a
Trafford book, or make use of our publishing services. To find out how you are
helping, please visit www.trafford.com/responsiblepublishing.html*

*Our mission is to efficiently provide the world's finest, most comprehensive
book publishing service, enabling every author to experience success.
To find out how to publish your book, your way, and have it available
worldwide, visit us online at www.trafford.com/10510*

 www.trafford.com

North America & international
toll-free: 1 888 232 4444 (USA & Canada)
phone: 250 383 6864 ♦ fax: 250 383 6804 ♦ email: info@trafford.com

The United Kingdom & Europe
phone: +44 (0)1865 487 395 ♦ local rate: 0845 230 9601
facsimile: +44 (0)1865 481 507 ♦ email: info.uk@trafford.com

10 9 8 7 6 5 4 3 2

Acknowledgements

This book has been nourished by many sources especially the hundreds of participants in workshops on the Heroic Journey. Continued exploration of the many paths of the Heroic Journey is my life work – my Opus.

Joseph Campbell is and will always be, one of my most treasured teachers. I hope that this small offering continues in the same spirit – to recognize and celebrate the Power of Myth. Campbell advised us to "follow our bliss." May this offering guide the way!

Carl Gustav Jung continues to inspire deeper questions and exploration into new territory – especially into the world of business. I find it a dangerous territory that demands heroic deeds. To change the world of business requires a working map towards possibility and potential. We need to revision the way we work and return to the power of the creative imagination.

Michael Ray, Lorna Catford, David Miller, Dennis Slattery, James Hillman, Marion Woodman, James Hollis and many other master storytellers too numerous to mention continue to act as mentors for my Journey. I gratefully build on their generous and creative spirits. Any errors or omissions are my own. Most importantly, this book is dedicated to students of life everywhere and in particular, to the students at Simon Fraser University in British Columbia, Canada.

When my soul is starving, you feed me.

The Threshold

There comes a time in your life when you stop for a moment and look around you at what you have accomplished. How far you have come. Where you might yet go.

All too often, that moment is not as joyful as you might have expected when you started to dream of your future. Most of us are not living the life we had planned, but instead, are living the life we are given. Life just seems to happen.

To use the language of myth, especially of the Heroic Journey, directs the mind and heart to the ultimate mystery that contains all existence. To use a mythic approach enables you to see what is just beyond your field of sight, to re-vision your relationship both personally and professionally. "Live" Nietzsche says "as though the day were here." Each individual must claim the power of his or her Heroic Journey. A mythic imagination can lead the way forward. But how?

This mythoi or little story, comes from the Grail. The Grail is the only myth where the heroic deed is an act of speech, so perhaps it is a fitting one for the problem at hand in finding an authentic voice.

The knight, Gawain, and the boys were out hunting. They had caught much game and wanted to make camp for the night and cook their dinner. They needed water for the cooking pots and one of the hunters said that he had spotted a well a little ways back in the forest. He volunteered to go fetch water for cooking and sauntered off.

As he approached the well, a hideous creature appeared before him. She was the ugliest, smelliest, wartiest, most disgusting creature he had ever the misfortune to lay eyes upon. She jumped in front of the well and demanded, "What do you want?" He replied, "If you please, I have come for water." She nodded. "Water you may have, but first you must kiss me." Horrified at this request, the hunter ran back to the group and told his tale of woe. The other hunters laughed at his discomfort and several others also made the attempt but with no success. The creature truly was terrible to behold and her request unbearable to contemplate.

Gawain in disgust watched his hunters fail repeatedly. Finally, he said, "I am a Knight. I will go and face this creature and get the water we need." He proceeded off into the forest and approached the well. Sure enough, the hag appeared. She jumped in front of the well and demanded, "What do you want?" He replied, "If you please, I have come for water." She nodded. "Water you may have, but first you must kiss me." Gawain did, and I must add, did a quite a thorough job indeed.

As you might have anticipated, the hag then turned into the most exquisite beauty he had ever seen. She smiled and said "You have won me by deed (which was the way of the times). Now choose. Do you wish my current shape for your pleasure at night and my other shape for your friends to admire during the day? Or, my current shape for your friends to envy during the day and my other shape for your pleasure at night?"

Gawain did not hesitate for he was a true Knight. He said, "My lady, the choice must be yours, for it is your body." She smiled sweetly and stated, "Dear Knight, you have not only named my heart's desire, but the desire of any one of us.

To hold the power to choose."

Mythologist Joseph Campbell instructed us to follow our bliss. To do so, you must claim your power to choose. Such an act involves risk, as you then become vulnerable to loss. Your choice might be refused. Your choice may be ridiculed. But, if you do not make it, you lose the passion for your profession. You may lose the passion for your life. Thus the importance of the Heroic Journey, as it provides a map for the territory of choice.

Never forget you have the power to choose. Choose your life. Pack light for the journey. Take a long look at yourself in the mirror. To embark on your own Heroic Journey is to embark on a path that will forever change you. Surrender your old life and walk towards the future. Ready?

Let us begin.

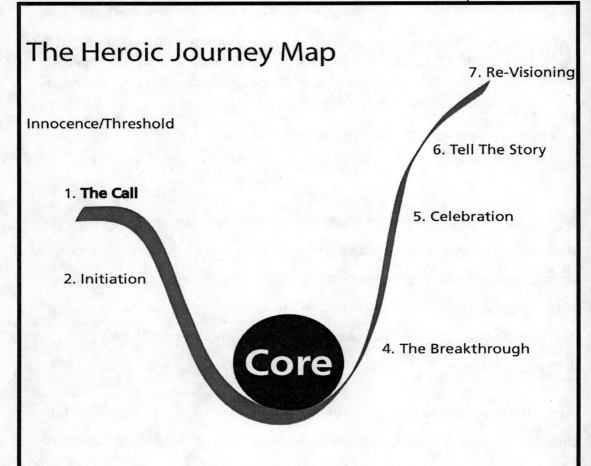

The Heroic Journey Map

Innocence/Threshold

1. **The Call**

2. Initiation

Core

4. The Breakthrough

5. Celebration

6. Tell The Story

7. Re-Visioning

Who or what is calling to you?

Are you refusing to answer?

Where are you feeling stuck in old patterns in your life?

What seems undone or unfinished?

What needs to be re-awakened?

Person? Place? Thing?

What happens when you slow down and listen?

Re-awaken your ability and creative potential to move confidently forward.

The Call and Relationship

We recommend that all readers begin the Heroic Journey workbook activities with this first step on the journey. James Hillman notes that he begins such work by inviting Psyche in, to be present and to guide in the work. Since the language of Psyche is image, and it comes from the terrain of the unconscious, I suggest that even if you have no idea why you are drawn to specific images, trust that there is a significant reason for an image or set of images stirring a response in you at this point. By the end of this journey there will be some clarity as to why these particular images or symbols spoke to you so loudly. Trust your intuition! and stay with your image.

Over the next days, or weeks, **collect** any images that appeal to you. These may be on junk mail flyers, postcards from stores and art galleries, pictures in magazines, newspapers, advertising, or work contexts. They may be favorite photos, images from hobbies such as crafts and fishing, or used stamps, labels, or calendars. If you have access to the Internet, search Flickr and see what images others have collected before you.

Choose one or two images that carry some emotion for you. How is your emotional response to the image associated with the idea of change, whether an imposed change or being called to attempt change in some way? If you have some idea of how they are connected, then write about that or talk with a trusted friend. Paste the image into your workbook or journal. Add any written information that you are comfortable including along with it.

Mythoi: A Long Time Ago, just Yesterday ...

In the time of Arthur and the Roundtable when a knight felt himself ready to venture forth on his Quest for the Grail, he went in search of Merlin for guidance. Merlin would take the knight to a place in the forest where there was no path. The terrified knight would gaze into the seemingly impenetrable forest and pray for guidance and strength to follow his Heart. To make a Quest is to conquer your own fear of the unknown. To make a Quest is to trust the wisdom within you to create a path that no one has ever walked before.

Whenever a knight of the Grail tried to follow a path made by someone else, he went altogether astray. Where there is a way or path, it is someone else's footsteps. Each of us has to find our own way.

Joseph Campbell

Myth-Making

Psyche always speaks. From this point onward, assume that you are willing to listen! To work within your own Heroic Journey means you need to construct a map, a path that you will follow in your Quest. The primary role of myth is to act as a bridge and to carry the past into the present and beyond. Myths provide us with the power to change – to demonstrate we have the power to choose.

The dictionary is the only place where success comes before work.

Arthur Brisbane

The Call and Recognition

If no image comes immediately to mind, here are some starter suggestions. If you don't know the answer, then pretend that you do! Record your answers in the book or in your Journal.

What is your favorite movie?

What is your favorite song?

What is your favorite painting?

What and where is your favorite place?

What country or location would you like to visit?

Do you have a favorite book, story, fairytale or myth from childhood?

What is your favorite animal?

Who is your own personal Hero/ine?

In your journal, record your image – that which calls you to follow. Where is yet unknown, as it should be. If you do not know why such an image speaks to you, you have chosen wisely. Go beyond the limits of your own logic, your own rational mind, to the place of myth-making – your own creative centre. You are about to begin your life as a work of art. Your life is the canvas and your potential is limited only by your imagination, your ability to re-vision.

   The unexamined life is not worth living.

Plato

Sentence Stems

Complete these sentence stems with whatever first comes to mind. The more spontaneous the better!

When I think of making a major life change I

One of the biggest comforts in my present life is

When I think of living the rest of my life like I am now, then I feel

To me security is

The status quo

Some of my strongest relationships

I yearn for

The biggest change I expect to make in the next five years is

The most obvious roles I carry in my life now are

Another role I have most people don't know about is

The role I find the least fulfilling is

One role I'd love to carry but don't have yet is

Previous Calls

Make a list of three Calls you've received in the past. These may be challenges offered by a teacher or coach, an invitation from a friend, or an opportunity you were told about. They may even be related to a time you moved to a new location, or when you or a family member had an accident or became very ill. They can include a new job-skill, sport, or activity that you chose to tackle. After you list the Calls, write down what you now remember were your thoughts and your feelings back then, as you considered answering – or refusing – each Call.

Call # 1.

Thoughts:

Feelings:

Call # 2.

Thoughts:

Feelings:

Call # 3.

Thoughts:

Feelings:

The hero, therefore, is the man or woman who has been able to battle past his personal and local historical limitations.

Joseph Campbell

Go to The Movies

Watch one or more of the following movies, noting specifically what the Call is for the main character(s). In fact I suggest that as you watch the movies, have a map of the Heroic Journey with you, and make a brief note of events that mark the transition into each new phase of the journey. This would also make an excellent Roundtable discussion for some friends with like minds, especially when the weather turns cold. Good food, good friends, good discussion!

Some of my recent favorites that I watch whenever I need food for my soul:

It's a Wonderful Life (my Christmas favorite!)
Star Wars series (the first three)
The Lion King
Matrix
Finding Neverland
Finding Nemo
Out of Africa
The Last Samurai
Million Dollar Baby
Erin Brockovich
Thelma and Louise
American President
Munich
Crash
The Chronicles of Narnia (one of my all-time favorites! including the book series)

Watch TV

Pick your favorite TV show. Each week what are the characters called to undertake? What is new? Notice what your favorite character is called to do and how he or she responds. What appeals to you about this character? What does this character have to say to you about finding your Call? Try using the Heroic Journey map again and see if the character speaks more fully to you.

A man's work is nothing more than to rediscover, through the detours of art, those one or two images in the presence of which his heart first opened.

Albert Camus

Don't Skip the Ads!

Think about which advertisements appeal to you. What products, if any, that you see advertised do you use? What draws you to use, or drive, these particular ones? What is it, in the image of the advertisement that calls to you?

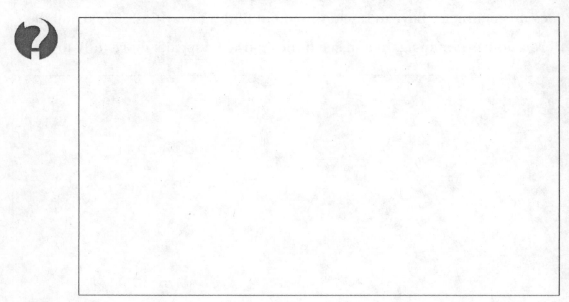

Curl Up With A Good Book...

Start reading myths and fairytales. When you are in a bookstore or library take a book on these topics off the shelf and open it at random. Read just one story. They are usually short, so just read it and notice whether the story resonates within you. If you have children, read original children's versions to them. Many picture books also have beautiful illustrations – images – to accompany the story. Even if you do not have children, read some of these picture book versions for yourself. If you can afford it, begin a collection of books of myths and fairytales.

Read at least four or five different stories, and more if you can! Make a note of which ones really resonate for you. Write down the name, and source, of the story. Although you will work with only one or two for now, the others may become significant in a few months or years. If you like, map the Heroic Journey of the story's character(s). Then sit back and think about the story. How this story is your story. Remember, you have chosen a story that has already resonated in your body, so there is some reality in it for your life. How are you living out this story in your day-to-day reality?

Practice Your Power to Choose

Try this simple exercise for the next week. Each day, pick someone whom you dislike. The next time you see them, complement them on an article of clothing. "Nice hat!" "Great tie!" and then keep walking. See what happens to your perception of that person. If this is just too hard, then pick a complete stranger in a restaurant or at a bus stop. Same instructions. Compliment them on what they are wearing and then keep on your way. What is the result? How does this affect your state of mind? What happens? What do you notice each day?

 I shut my eyes in order to see.

Paul Gauguin

Day One:

Day Two:

Day Three:

Day Four:

Day Five:

What have you learned?

The Call and Meaning

One way to find the meaning that you are seeking is to examine your values – what you believe to be worthwhile or desirable. Values help you find a sense of purpose and direction. On the next page, you will find a partial list of value words to stimulate your thinking. If any values seem missing, please insert them as you work through this particular exercise. Do not hurry as this exercise is the one that I have always found to be the most important to people. When you know what you value, you have the tools you need in order to chart your course. Circle the values that are important to you.

affluence	authority	
art	adventure	
authenticity	admiration	
achievement	advancement	
ambition		
beauty	belonging	
balance	best	
connection	career	
culture	credit	
comfort	clarity	
close friends	challenge	

control	creativity	
competition	conformity	
discipline	drama	
dominance		
energy	excellence	
education	equality	
entrepreneurship	enjoyment	
endurance	employment	
entertainment		
family	fame	
faith	freedom	
friendship	fun	
goodness	greatness	
happiness	health	
honesty	hard work	
hope	healing	
humor	humility	

harmony		
imagination	income	
individualism	independence	
industrious	impulsive	
inquisitive	integrity	
joy	justice	
kindness	kin	
love	laughter	
loyalty	leadership	
leisure		
meditation	mastery	
mentor	morality	
money	maturity	
modesty		
nurturance	need	

openness	order	
obedience	ownership	
peace	play	
philosophy		
pleasure	power	
persistence	politics	
professionalism	prosperity	
quality	quietness	
religion	recognition	
relationship	respect	
responsibility	rewards	
retirement	reputation	
riches	rebellion	
security	satisfaction	
sincerity	success	
space	spirituality	
survival	status	

teamwork	tradition	
tranquility	truth	
trust	tenacity	
technique	time	
travel		
wealth	wisdom	
winning	well-being	
work		
youth		
zeal	zest	

Values influence our decisions and help us determine which path is right for us at this point in time. Make a list of your top ten values:

1
2

3
4
5
6
7
8
9
10

Now write definitions for each of these values. You may choose to consult a dictionary. The important part is in finding the definition that speaks to you, that best defines what you mean by each of these values. Next, find an image that expands or elaborates what each of these values mean to you. Be as specific as you can. When you 'picture something in your mind', you draw on the power of your imagination.

 Everyone has been called for some particular work, and the desire for that work has been put in his heart.

Rumi

Archetypal Tri-Model: Individual

Meaning – What you Take to Believe
Who is myself?
What is my opus (my life's work)?

Individual
Recognition
Relationship
Meaning

Recognition of Self
Individual Strengths
Values-driven (archetypal)
Communication Styles
Leadership Potential
Espoused Values

Core

Relationship to Others
Values-driven (archetypal)
Values in action
Maximize Leadership -
walk the talk

Write your obituary – as a celebration of your life.

What would your life partner say about you?
What would your children say about you?
What would your friends say about you?
What would your co-workers and business partners say about you?
What would your parents say about you?
What would your neighbours say about you?

Post your 'celebration of life' on your fridge in the kitchen. How do friends/
family respond to your claims? Do you need to make any adjustments?

After reflection and discussion with friends and family, make a shorter list.

My legacy

I want to be remembered for:

Treat this as further fuel to add to your Call. Are you livinig your life to the
fullest? If you want to be remembered as you have listed, start now! What do
you need to do?

Make a list of ten words or phrases that describe you best. They might be functions, activities, affiliations or feelings (I am punctual, reliable, chief marketing officer, female, middle-aged, member of the Better Business Bureau, competent, loyal, etc.)

I am
I am
I am
I am
I am
I am
I am
I am
I am
I am

How much of your self image is shaped by stereotypes or roles that you play? How do these descriptions match with your ten top values? Are you living your values at work?

 If you are called to be a street sweeper, sweep streets even as Michelangelo painted, or Beethoven composed music, or Shakespeare wrote poetry. Sweep streets so well that all the hosts of heaven and earth will pause to say, "Here lived a great street sweeper who did his job well."

Martin Luther King, Jr.

Personal Strategic Plan

Packing for the Journey (behaviors I wish to change)	Threshold Guardians (who or what stands in my way?)	Allies (who or what can help me on my journey?)	When By? (set a date to accomplish this task)

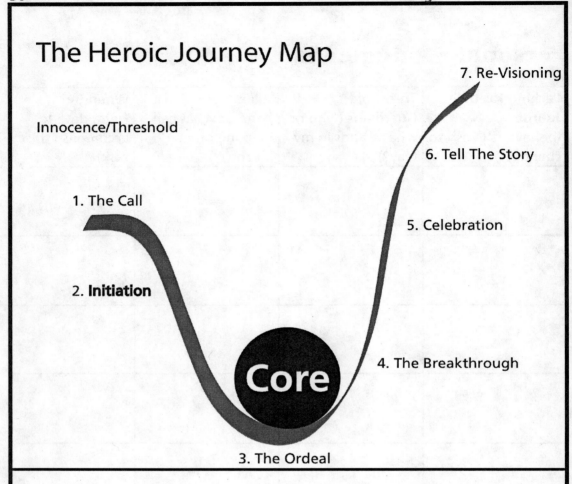

The Heroic Journey Map

Innocence/Threshold

1. The Call

2. **Initiation**

3. The Ordeal

Core

4. The Breakthrough

5. Celebration

6. Tell The Story

7. Re-Visioning

In proceeding with your new way of thinking and believing, what problems did you encounter?

What rites of passage are you ignoring?

What threshold guardians or enemies block your way?

Emotional support from others? No support?

How did you protect the development of your new ideas from initial criticism? (a normal response to proposed change).

Initiation

 A man has many skins in himself, covering the depths of his heart. Man knows so many things; he does not know himself. Why, thirty or forty skins or hides, just like an ox's or a bear's, so thick and hard, cover the soul. Go into your own ground and learn to know yourself there.

Meister Eckhart

When you realize you need to change the course of your life path, it may feel overwhelming.

To claim the power to choose, first you must claim your Self, the Self that has become covered in the hides of routine and responsibility.

 One of the problems women have today is that they are not willing to find the river in their own life and surrender to its current. They are not willing to spend time discovering themselves, because they feel they are being selfish. They grow up trying to please other people and they rarely ask themselves, who am I? Rarely. And then life starts to feel meaningless because they live in terms of pleasing, rather than in terms of being who they are.

Marion Woodman

Initiation and Relationship

It is time to make a promise, to set a course for a new beginning.

Take the image from your Personal Myth and create a small sanctuary in honor of that image. Remember that image may come from any of the senses. From whichever sense your image came to you, honor also the other senses that support it (smell, taste, touch, sight, sound).

You are going to create an intention. Not a goal – that comes later. Intentionality is a state of being, not doing. Focus now on being and what is within you to become. The word intention comes from the Latin root intendere meaning to turn one's attention in – toward + tendere – to stretch. As previously stated – to initiate, means to begin or originate, and is commonly used as a verb, meaning to introduce some knowledge or practice. You are going to create a practice that will support your Quest. Such a practice takes time as you will need to reflect on your choices.

 There is more to life than increasing its speed.

Gandhi

Mythoi: A Long Time Ago, just Yesterday ...

Uncertainty is common in periods of transition. Being aware of our conscious part in creating a new story gives us greater control over how these transitions affect us.

 The "eye of initiation," the way of looking through one's life to see where the initiatory breaks occur, requires reimagining one's own biography.

Michael Meade

Myth-Making

When we set our intention for this new beginning, we begin to form the new foundation on which to build. Again, incorporate the gender and ancient wisdom of your body. Using the power of archetypal psychology you can create a temenos or container, by asking your Self some more questions about your previous Quest Questions. Go deeper into your answers. Like the skin of an onion, peel away superficial layers and deepen your responses. Whichever of the questions called to you, re-visit your immediate reply.

Initiation and Recognition

In your favorite movie, what characters appealed to you? Why? Watch the movie again. What more do you see? What additional components of the character(s)?

In your favorite song, what words struck you most deeply? Why? What longing is communicated? Where do you hunger?

What work(s) of art move you? Look deeper into the image. What is there that you did not see before? What additional teachings are contained within the work of art?

Gather images of your favorite place. What calls to you from this location? Why this location and not some other? What is different? How are you different?

What is the appeal of the country or location you would like to visit? Why are you drawn there?

What are the attributes of your favorite animal? Are those attributes at play in your own life or are they missing?

What is your favorite book or myth or story or fairytale from childhood? Why this one and not another?

What are the attributes of your favorite Hero/ine? Do you aspire to these characteristics? Do you possess these characteristics already but are somehow blocked from accessing them?

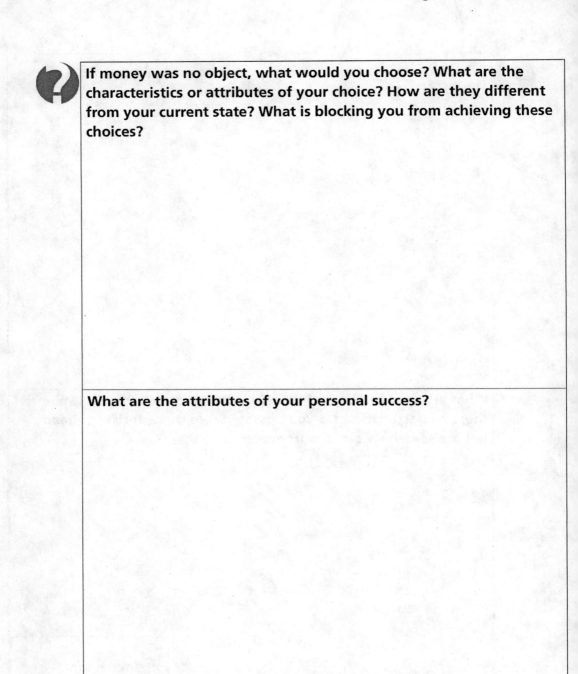

If money was no object, what would you choose? What are the characteristics or attributes of your choice? How are they different from your current state? What is blocking you from achieving these choices?

What are the attributes of your personal success?

Checking In:
How do you feel right now? Are you comfortable with these
questions and your responses? Why or why not?

Is there a pattern in your responses?

Is there a critical voice that interrupts your musings? What does it look like?

Does it remind you of anyone you know? Take a few moments and draw this

voice.

My critical voice

Practice Your Power to Choose

Who do you want in your life? You might not be able to choose your circumstances and the people associated with those circumstances, but you can choose your response.

You have the beginning of this list of characteristics, attributes, values that you hold dear. Consider these the price of admission to your life. Who do you wish to admit?

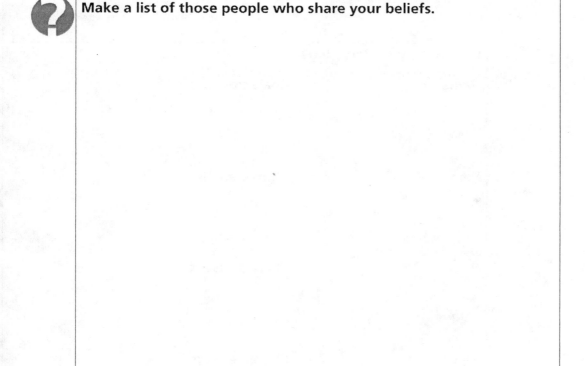

Make a list of those people who share your beliefs.

Are there any values that are not in abundance? Make a list of those values you wish to draw into your daily life.

I admire people who

I wish to spend more time with people who

I like people who

Whom are you attracting?

Name	Characteristics

Name	Characteristics

Name	Characteristics

Name	Characteristics

The people in our life can sometimes act as a mirror. When you look outside your life, what do you see? The function of initiation is to mark a place of transition — from one type of life to another. When you consciously use your power to choose, you can look deeply into the mirror and see your reflection. In order to change, you must act. What actions do you see you need to make?

Writes of Passage

Write your life to date as a story. Are you a hero or a victim? How have you celebrated your rites of passage? How have you exercised your power to choose? Or have you? Whose life have you been living?

My Story as a Fairy Tale

Once upon a time, just yesterday there lived...

We enter the territory of the heart by going into our wounds and reliving them. By 'wounds' I mean those blows from life that stun and injure one's spirit, that lacerate and mark the tissues of the soul.

Michael Meade

Previous Initiations

Make a list of three Initiations you have survived in the past. What happened? What caused the initiation? After you list the Initiations, write down what you now remember were your thoughts and your feelings back then, as you considered answering – or refusing – each Initation.

Initiation # 1

Thoughts:

Feelings:

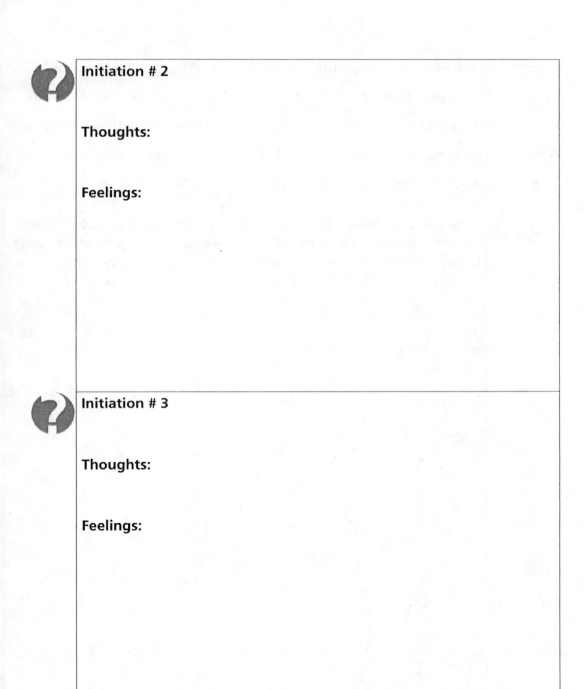

Initiation # 2

Thoughts:

Feelings:

Initiation # 3

Thoughts:

Feelings:

Remember the advertisements that appeal to you. What products, if any, that you see advertised do you use? What draws you to use, or drive, these particular ones? What is it, in the image of the advertisement that calls to you? Have you changed your purchase based on your discovery? Do you notice yourself being attracted to something you were not before?

 Only you can change the ending of this story. What initiation ritual can you construct for yourself that marks the beginning of the your transition from old life to new? Rituals are meaning in action.

Your Tribe

There is not an I without a We. Each of us was shaped by our past. To know yourself is to see where family rules, regulations, customs, traditions, taboos and rituals influence your behavior. Some still serve you well. Some do not.

It is only when we consciously look at "the way things are done around here," that we can see what is still valued and what needs to be left behind. Every parent has felt the disconnect between what is ideal and actual. Sometimes the messages given are contradictory. Every child has witnessed the difference between what is said and what is done.

Generally speaking, all the life which the parents could have lived, but of which they thwarted themselves for artificial motives, is passed on to the children in substitute form... The children are driven unconsciously in a direction that is intended to compensate for everything that was left unfulfilled in the lives of the parents.

C.G. Jung

What are your family "Rules"? The "shoulds"? The "everybody knows"? ("You should always eat everything on your plate." "You should always shine your shoes." "Everyone knows that work and pleasure are separate things." "You can't make a living doing (pick something you enjoy!!)" "Mind your manners! (which ones??)" "Don't be selfish!" You get the idea. What slogans or clichés were repeated over and over in your family until they became fact instead of opinion?

In order to move into your future, you need to pack. I suggest you pack light. What traditions do you keep and what do you give away or leave behind? What are the unconscious messages hidden in your family's oral tradition?

Rule/Tradition/Taboo	Keep	Give Away

The most conscientious way to honor one's father and mother is to "leave" them; to accept and understand with gratitude, what has come through them and to take those motifs to their next level of expression.

Linda Sussman

Our first ideas of how a "woman" should behave and how a "man" should behave come from our first examples. Usually, they are your parents but can also include any formative person in your young life.

You and your Mother (or other Mother figure) – Introduction to The Feminine

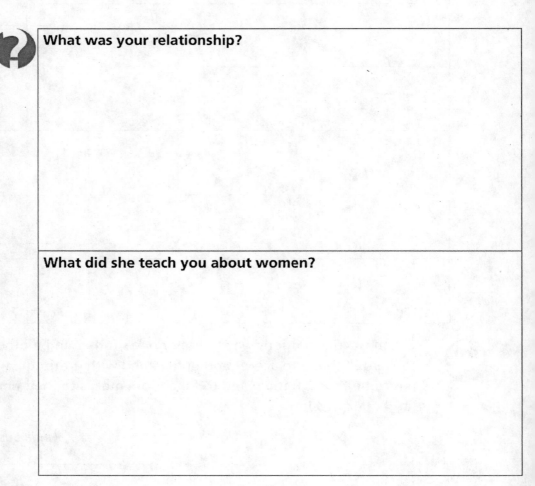

What was your relationship?

What did she teach you about women?

What did she teach you about men?

What are her values that you hold dear?

What are her values that you reject?

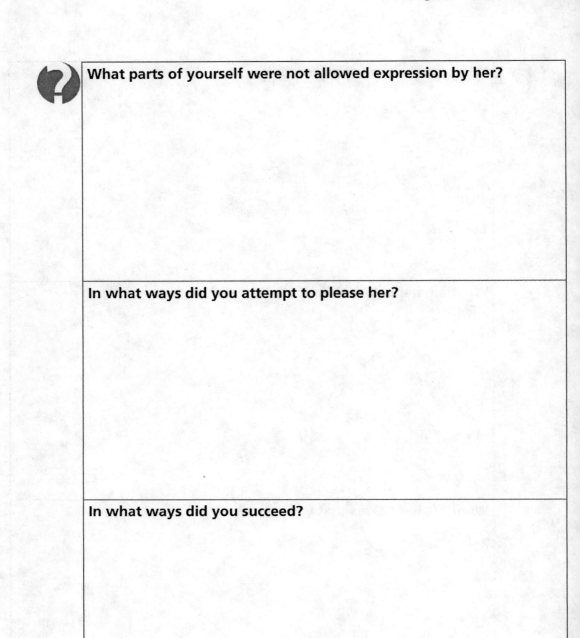

What parts of yourself were not allowed expression by her?

In what ways did you attempt to please her?

In what ways did you succeed?

In what ways did you fail?

What does the voice of your mother say inside your head?

Did you have other female mentors?

What image of the feminine do you carry?

You and your Father (or other Father figure) – Introduction to The Masculine

 What was your relationship?

What did he teach you about men?

What did he teach you about women?

What are his values that you hold dear?

What are his values that you reject?

What parts of yourself were not allowed expression by him?

In what ways did you attempt to please him?

In what ways did you succeed?

In what ways did you fail?

What does the voice of your father say inside your head?

Did you have other male mentors?

What image of the masculine do you carry?

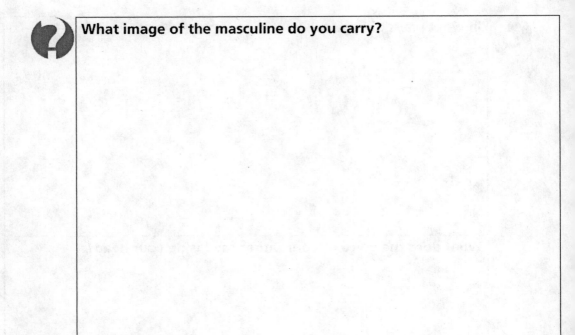

The truth about the need for heroes is not easy for anyone to admit... To become conscious of what one is doing to earn his feeling of heroism is the main self-analytic problem of life. Everything painful and sobering in what psychoanalytic genius and religious genius have discovered about man revolves around the terror of admitting what one is doing to earn his self-esteem.

Ernest Becker

Your Favorite Teacher

Who is your favorite teacher? Living or dead. Human or not. What are his/her characteristics that made him/her such a great teacher? A teacher that you love. A teacher that you would spend time with for any reason.

Characteristics:

Teachers can also act as mirrors for the parts of your Self that are yet undeveloped or unexpressed. The characteristics that you admire are those that are unawakened in your Self. Can you incorporate these untapped talents into your Initiation?

Make a list of the aspects of your life that you identify with most
strongly, those that you wish to enhance and grow. Link those
characteristics from your favorite teachers to aspects of your life
you wish to enhance. For example, if your Grade 4 teacher was
incredibly patient with you and you wish to become a better mother
to your children or a better partner to your loved one, how could you
incorporate patience on a daily basis?

Characteristic of teacher i.e. patience	Aspect of my life i.e. better partner

For the next week, consciously practice each characteristic on a daily basis. Look for those opportunities presented to you to practice your power to choose.

All severe separations in life evoke the sense of initiation in the psyche and open a person to psychological and mythical territories of unusual depth. Initiation is the psyche's response to mystery, great difficulties, and opportunities to change.

Michael Meade

Initiation and Meaning

Perhaps in no other aspect of life is the act of initiation more needed. In making a shift from the old state to a new state of being, rites of passage provide structure in any tribe or culture. The importance of a guide or mentor is invaluable in navigating the unspoken aspects of a culture. More than just verbal guidance, the wisdom imparted by the mentor to the initiate enables the new member of the tribe to learn both the spoken and unspoken rules and regulations of tribal life. As Jung once remarked: "The mere use of words is futile if you do not know what they stand for." Use your chosen values and how you have defined them to provide a framework for guidance. And then go in search of a Mentor to aid your journey.

Initiation and Mentors

The concept of Mentor is an ancient one. In ancient India, the God Krishna advises General Arjuna on the battlefield, at the onset of the battle recounted in the Mahabharata. The advice Krishna provided became the Bhagavad Gita, which is a sacred text of Hinduism still used today. In ancient China, the wisdom of Lau Tsu provided the Tao, the Way, which is also still much in use. Thousands of years later in ancient Greece, the Goddess of Wisdom, Athena, disguised herself as a manservant named Mentor. She appeared to Telemachus, son of Odysseus, to advise him to go in search of his father. European court jesters served the purpose of truth-telling to the King. No one else dared to speak for fear of retaliation. The Jester or Court Fool provided guidance usually mixed with a good dose of humor that allowed the message to be more easily heard. Throughout the ages, to have a mentor was a priceless gift. Think back...

What mentors do you have available to you?

What mentors do you actively choose?

What actions will you take to invite the mentors you need to accompany you on your Journey?

Can you make those actions into a ritual that also supports your transition into Initiation? Can the mentor provide some assistance in taking those steps? Ask your mentor for a different lens by which to see the Journey. What happens?

 When you change the way you look at things ...the things you look at change.

David Bohm

The Heroic Journey Map

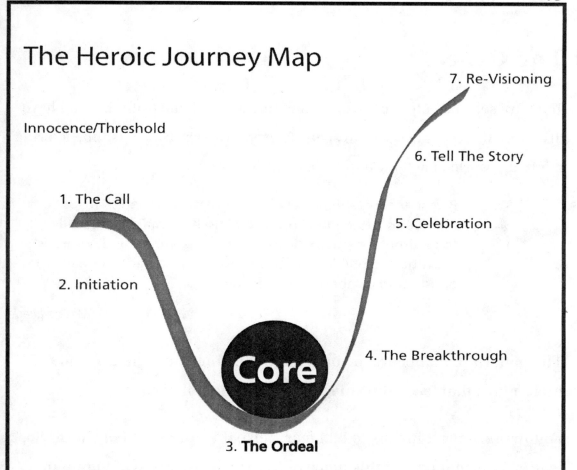

Innocence/Threshold

1. The Call

2. Initiation

3. **The Ordeal**

Core

4. The Breakthrough

5. Celebration

6. Tell The Story

7. Re-Visioning

Any major life change produces uncertainty during transition to a new way of thinking and believing.

What challenges do you fear?

What uninvited life changes have been imposed on you?

What roadblocks are you encountering?

Any ones that you did not anticipate? (This is usually the place you wake up at 3am and wonder if you are doing the right thing or have completely lost your mind!)

The Ordeal

You have set your intention. Now is the time to speak the truth that you have discovered. You are learning to speak from your heart. Now it is time to bring it into the world of action. Your ordeal has begun.

 Psychoanalysis still preserves the initiatory pattern. The patient is asked to descend deeply into himself, to make his past live, to confront his traumatic experiences again... This dangerous operation resembles initiatory descents into hell, the realm of ghosts, and combats with monsters.

Mircea Eliade

The pattern that appears to you from reviewing your images, and imaginings that feed your images can now be followed.

Following a quest means to feel fear...else it would not be a Quest! So, fear is a normal part of this place of Ordeal. If you are waking up in the middle of the night in a cold sweat, wondering if you have done the right thing; this is the place of the Ordeal. Your commitment to the Journey you have embarked upon is being tested.

 Life is either an adventure, or it is nothing.

Helen Keller

The Ordeal and Relationship

Over the next days, or weeks, return to your images that you collected from the Call. Group them into five sections: What? Where? How? Why Now? Why Me? Now is the time to find your voice. To speak your truth, but always with compassion.

When you are attempting to discover what actions you need to take, and get stuck on how to start, return to your images. If you want to find your dream job, dream relationship, dream anything, first you need to know who you are. That is the secret of the Ordeal. You might have spent your entire life living someone else's idea of who you are and what you should be doing. The Ordeal takes us into unexplored territory – our internal search for Self. In the search for Self, we rediscover our Creative Core.

Now is the time to find your voice. To speak your truth, but always with compassion. Make a list of current situations where you are silent but, you know you should speak. These situations could be at work, at home, at play. With colleagues or with friends or family. Find the compassion within to speak your truth in a way that maintains relationship with the other but does not compromise the relationship with your Self.

Situation	Why I Should Speak Up:	What I Would Say:

 The moment we begin to fear the opinions of others and hesitate to tell the truth that is in us, and from motives of policy are silent when we should speak, the divine floods of light and life no longer flow into our souls.

Elizabeth Cady Stanton

What happened when you found your voice? What teachings did you receive?

What was I Given?

This exercise is a simple one. What came in and what came out. What you put in are your fear, your struggles, your challenges, your obstacles, your problems, your setbacks and disappointments. Use specific personal or business situations and events.

What you generate are gifts, lessons, strengths, skills, experiences, understanding, insight, and wisdom. Again, be as specific as you can. One angle that may help is the phrase "So that next time, I was able to..."

Jump right in and work the machine below with your reflections:

Input	Output

Your vision will become clear only when you look into your heart. Who looks outside, dreams. Who looks within, awakens.

Carl Jung

The Power to Choose my Path Exercise:

Left Path-Make a list of all the things you think you should do:

Right Path -Now, make a list of the things you long to do, the things that are almost too delicious to consider.

Which path do you choose to follow?

 Don't ask yourself what the world needs.

Ask yourself what makes you come alive,

and then go do it.

Because what the world needs

is people who have come alive.

Howard Thurman

Mythoi: A Long Time Ago, just Yesterday ...

Using the images you have collected, write a story in the third person about you and finding the courage to speak.

Don't be satisfied with stories, how things have gone with others. Unfold your own myth.

Rumi

Myth-Making

You have created an intention and found your true voice. Now you are beginning to see how you have created your own myth – your story that you tell others and most importantly, tell to your Self.

One of the most painful parts of the Ordeal is learning to trust your Self. To collaborate with your Self. To honor your Self. To listen to your Self. In order for you to trust your Self, you will need to create a place of safety to continue to journey forward. Know that the journey has a destination and that the ordeal is the price you pay for the boon on the other side.

 I know God will not give me anything I can't handle. I just wish that He didn't trust me so much.

Mother Teresa

The Ordeal and Recognition

Recognition can be painful. When you map out your life to date, it is easy to focus on the mistakes along the way. Gifts and wounds are part of what makes us human. Both are universals in our lifetime. Paradoxically, one person's wound can be another person's gift. Part of the work of the Journey is healing the wounds already received and moving forward. There is no easy way to heal old wounds. A magic pill would be welcome (if you know of one, please let me know)! Otherwise, each person explores this territory and finds the tools for transformation within. Your creative core is the source for your healing, thus the importance of this Journey.

"Writes" of Passage

Complete these sentence stems with whatever first comes to mind. The more spontaneous the better!

What am I avoiding?

What am I ready to accept?

I am stuck because?

I am afraid of ?

What allies surround me?

What threshold guardians are blocking my way?

What do I fear most about them?

What will comfort me in this part of the Journey?

What strengths do I possess that are not being used?

Think of your personal Hero/ines! What do they possess and carry for you that you do not own?

Without this playing with fantasy no creative work has ever come to birth. The debt we owe to the play of imagination is uncalculable.

C.G. Jung

Previous Ordeals

Make a list of three Ordeals you have survived in the past. These may be challenges that were presented to you over the course of your life so far. What were your initial thoughts about the Ordeal? After you list the Ordeal, write down what you now remember were your thoughts and your feelings as you moved through the Ordeal. How did you survive? What coping skills did you use?

Ordeal # 1 **Thoughts:** **Feelings:**
Ordeal # 2 **Thoughts:** **Feelings:**
Ordeal # 3 **Thoughts:** **Feelings:**

The future enters into us, in order to transform itself in us, long before it happens.

Rainer Maria Rilke

Checking In

How do you feel right now? Are you comfortable with these questions and your responses? Why or why not?

Is there a pattern in your responses? Is there an Ordeal you have repeated? Same situation but different face or location?

Identify the physical and emotional ordeals you have experienced during your lifetime. What disappointments? What dreams unfulfilled? How have you coped with these losses?

Stage of	Challenge	How I Handled	Outcome
Early Childhood			
School Years			
Young Adult			
Now			
Later?			

Are you seeing any more patterns? Do you have typical ways you respond to challenges?

Only the wounded healer, heals.

T.S. Eliot

Practice Your Power To Choose

Ritual is a powerful ally in your Ordeal. In the last section, you identified who you wanted to keep in your life. Your allies can assist you in conducting rituals, if you feel that their presence would be of aid to help you move forward, and keep going on your Journey.

Making Sacred Bundles

For this ritual, you will need strips of cloth or paper, pens, and your favorite color of yarn or ribbon.

Write down the repetitive patterns you see in your life. Which ones no longer serve you? Which ones need to be discarded? left behind? What disappointments are you willing to let go? What associations make you smaller? less of yourself?

 ... anything or anyone that does not bring you alive is too small for you.

David Whyte

As David Whyte suggests, we treasure anything or anyone that feeds our growth. For anything or anyone who does not, why are you still carrying that particular bundle? These are the losses that weigh you down. Bundle up your losses and tie them together with your ribbon or yarn and set them aside.

What are the teachings you received from these life lessons? Write these teachings down as well and make a separate bundle.

Ritual

Either with your allies or alone, create your own ritual around disposing the bundle that no longer serves you. You may burn it. You may bury it. You may cast it into the wind. Understand that you are now willing to release these losses and will not pick them up again.

Either with your allies or alone, now speak aloud the teachings you gained, the gifts received. Claim these gifts as your own. Speak aloud how you will bring them on your Journey.

 All sorrows can be borne if you put them into a story or tell a story about them.

Isak Dinesen

Your Path to Purpose

Take a moment now and return to the movie of your own life. Put yourself in the place of the Hero (for who else could play you?). How do these gifts you have received enable you to move forward? How do these gifts relate to the core of your own being? What have you learned?

Never underestimate the power of story. Rent or watch the movie " Life is Beautiful". How does writing your own story reflect the message of the movie? How do you interpret your life events to date? Can you see them through a different lens? What happens if you do?

Visual Hero Map

Where I am at the start of this Journey:

Date:

7. Re-Visioning

Innocence/Threshold

6. Tell The Story

1. The Call

5. Celebration

2. Initiation

Core

4. The Breakthrough

3. The Ordeal

Writes of Passage: Path to Purpose

Threshold: (how I feel about my situation)
The Call to Adventure: (what is my challenge?)
Threshold Guardians: (who blocks my way?)
Initiation: (how am I tested?)
Allies: (who guides me?)
Ordeal: (what needs to be accomplished?)
Breakthrough: (reaching new awareness?)
Celebration: (how? with who?)
Telling the Story: (what gifts are you bringing home with you?)
Re-Visioning: (how is your life different?)

The Ordeal and Meaning

Review what you have learned so far. You are finding what is most valuable to you. What you love to do also feeds the Journey and holds untapped wisdom for the road ahead. What do you love to do?

	Things I Love To Do
1	
2	
3	
4	
5	
6	
7	
8	
9	
10	
11	
12	
13	
14	

Finding Your Creative Core

Return to the section where you circled your most important values. In order to find your creative core, the values that you hold most dear can be used to build your Path to Purpose. In each of the circles below, insert one value. Limit your selection to your top five values.

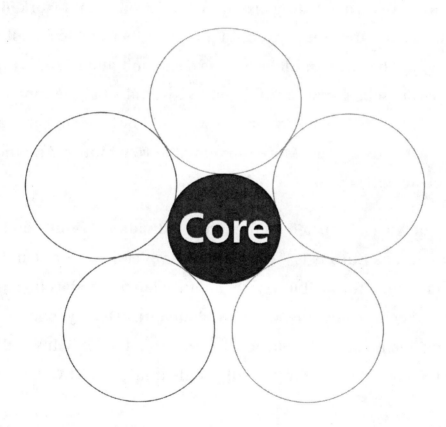

What People Think

Don't do _____, what will people say? This exercise will help you find out and isolate who these "people" are that "everybody" keeps referring to as such an authority in your life. Who is everybody? Who are these people? Should you even care? Let's find out.

I remember years ago sitting around with a group that I worked with. I don't remember the company, but I do remember the people. It was at a time when the cure for all bad jobs was to quit and go to Europe and discover yourself. Every day at lunch, we would sit in the lunch room, bemoan our lot in life and wish that we could quit our job and go to Europe. All of us agreed. More moaning. More whining. And then ... someone actually did it!

Immediately we all turned on the lucky individual. "Don't you know how dangerous Europe is"? (forgetting completely how much we all wanted to go). "You will never get another job as good as this one" (forgetting completely how much we hated it). "Don't you know how irresponsible it is to quit your job?" (forgetting how much we all wanted to do just that). "What will people think?" (WHAT PEOPLE?).

Writes of Passage: Who Are These People?

Everybody hates it when I...
Everybody loves it when I...
Everybody knows that if you _____ _____will happen
Nobody gets away with...
Everybody expects me to...
When I am successful, people...
When I fail, people...
People judge me when I...

For each statement above, write the names of everybody who believes the statement. Everybody!! Can you come up with more than five names? Everybody!!

Just who are 'these people' and why are they in your life? Why are you listening?

Don't be upset if some of the 'people' you list are members of your family. Your family doesn't fully know what is in your creative core. If they did, you wouldn't be looking for it now.

Who Feeds You?

In each of the circles below, insert the names of those who 'feed' you.
Who feeds your need for relationship? Who feeds your sense of self?
Who feeds your creative core? Who shares your values? Who feeds your
need to be recognized, your accomplishments, your good deeds, your
talents, your untapped potential? Who enriches and adds meaning to
your life?

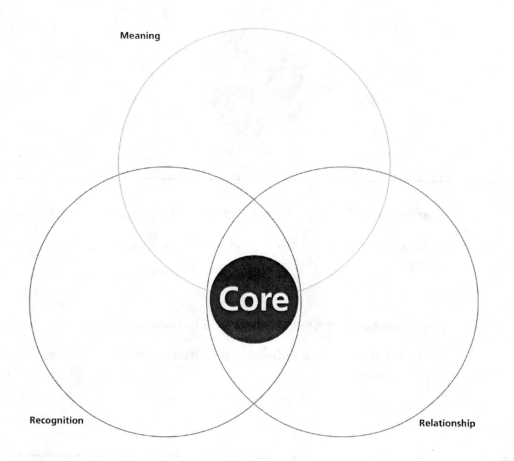

The Heroic Journey Map

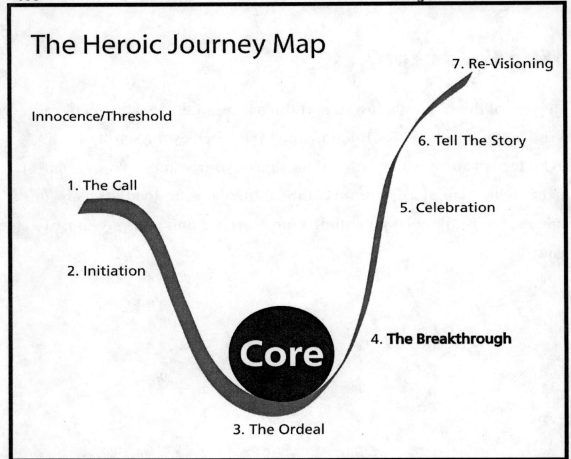

Innocence/Threshold

1. The Call

2. Initiation

3. The Ordeal

Core

4. **The Breakthrough**

5. Celebration

6. Tell The Story

7. Re-Visioning

As some people begin to see the benefit of change, they embrace it.

As your new way of thinking proceeds, has your support system changed?

How?

What "ah hah!" moments have you experienced?

How might you have extinguished the frequency of these opportunities?

Breakthrough and Relationship

When you are questioning your very existence, those questions that begin with "how" are usually less intimidating that those that begin with "why". How or what tends to ask for a description where why tends to ask for an explanation or a reason. When you are questioning others in your family, friends or workplace, avoid asking why questions when emotions are running high. When you are exploring your own personal values, as you shift so will your relationship to others. Some people will find this disturbing!

Mythoi: The Good Old Days...

What were the good old days like?

What do you miss about the way things used to be?

What have you learned that you are glad to see gone?

Is there a way to keep some of the good things from the past? What could you do to bring the best of the past forward into the present?

Leave Behind

What needs to be left behind if you are going to survive the journey?

What things might other people want to keep, that you have decided to leave behind? How might you tell them of your plans in a way that acknowledges their attachment?

What can happen if people try and carry everything along with them on this journey?

The Essentials: Packing Light

What are the essentials - what have you learned are the requirements for making it through this journey?

Do you have them? If not, can you develop them?

How can you develop these skills?

Breakthrough and Recognition

As you review what you have done to this point, it is important to recognize the distance you have traveled. Go back once again to the images you have collected. Sit with them once more and review each image. Go back once again to the values you have claimed as your own.

How do your images and values link together?

What did you notice?

Anything that jumped into clear view?

What is your gut reaction to what you have noticed?

Is there a favorite or recurring theme?

What would this insight look like if it were better managed?

What changes would take place in your current lifestyle?

What patterns of behavior would be in place that are not currently?

What would you have that you do not have now?

What would you be doing differently with the people in your life?

Sentence Stems

Complete these sentence stems with whatever first comes to mind. The more spontaneous the better! SCAMPER is a technique used in organizational development, but it works just as well with personal situations.

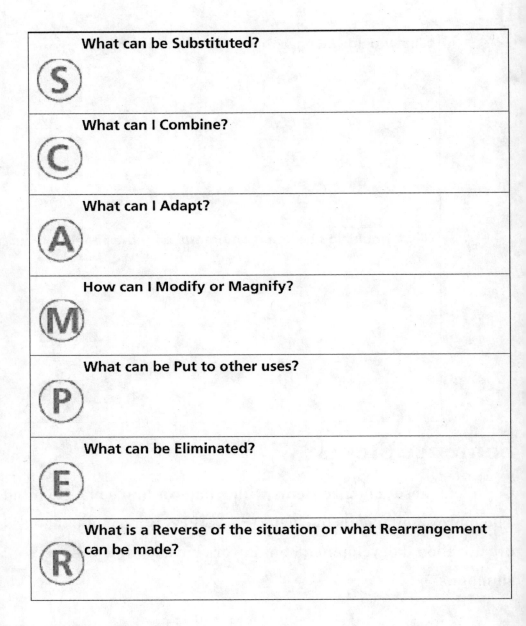

(S)	**What can be Substituted?**
(C)	**What can I Combine?**
(A)	**What can I Adapt?**
(M)	**How can I Modify or Magnify?**
(P)	**What can be Put to other uses?**
(E)	**What can be Eliminated?**
(R)	**What is a Reverse of the situation or what Rearrangement can be made?**

Previous Breakthroughs

Make a list of significant Breakthroughs you have experienced in the past. How did these insights come to you? After you list the

Breakthrough, write down what you now remember were your thoughts and your feelings back then. How intense was the realization? What coping skills did you use to implement your hard-won insight?

Breakthrough # 1

Thoughts:

Feelings:

Breakthrough # 2

Thoughts:

Feelings:

Breakthrough # 3

Thoughts:

Feelings:

Is there an image that can signify your realizations? Take a few moments and draw, paint or otherwise insert this image.

Archetypal Tri-Model: Tribes

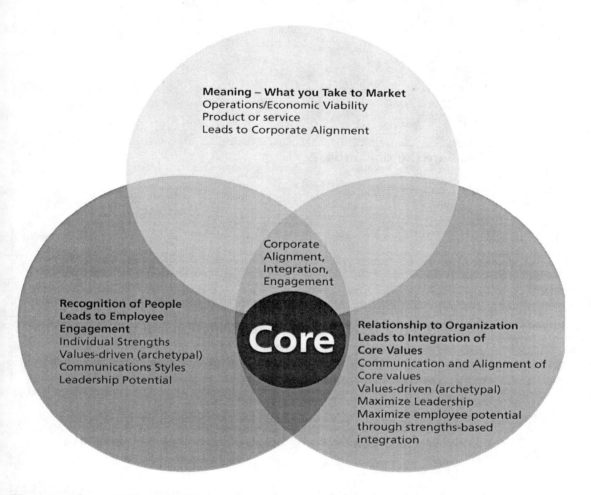

Practice Your Power to Choose

Which generation do you belong to? Who is your tribe? Do these various stages speak to you? Find another who is of the same generation and talk about what you value and how you describe it.

What are the differences?

What are the similarities?

Find another who is of a different generation and talk about what you value and how you describe it.

What are the differences?

What are the similarities?

Breakthrough and Meaning

What stresses are in place? What needs to be shifted or changed in order for you to realize on your breakthroughs?

Current areas of stress	1	
	2	
	3	
	4	
1: Stress that requires action (avoidable)	1	
	2	
	3	
2: Stress that needs greater clarity (avoidable-unavoidable)	1	
	2	
	3	
3: Stress that calls for development of a new philosophical attitude (unavoidable)	1	
	2	
	3	

Time Map

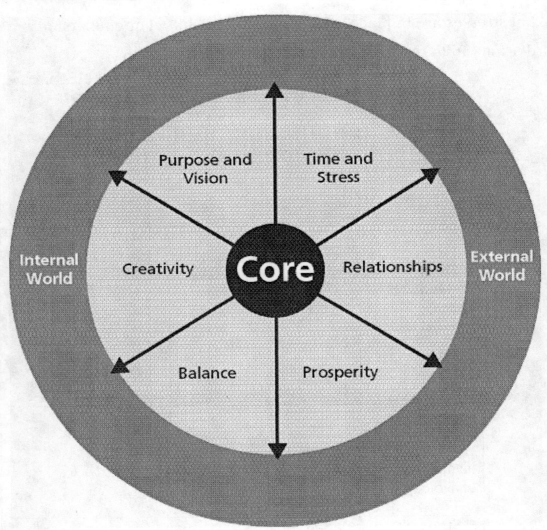

What percentages can you allocate to these areas of your life?

What have you noticed in your exploration so far that has changed in each of these areas of your life?

How has your realization changed your relationships?

What do you need or are willing to grieve for?

Say it out loud. I need to grieve for...

> **What have you finished grieving for?**

Say it out loud. I am finishing grieving for...

> **What are you still avoiding...because...?**

Say it out loud. I am still avoiding...because...

> **What are you still yearning for...because...?**

Say it out loud. I am still yearning for...because...

> **What gifts of grace are being offered to you?**

Say it out loud. I accept the gift of...

> **What is emerging in my life right now is ...**

The Heroic Journey Map

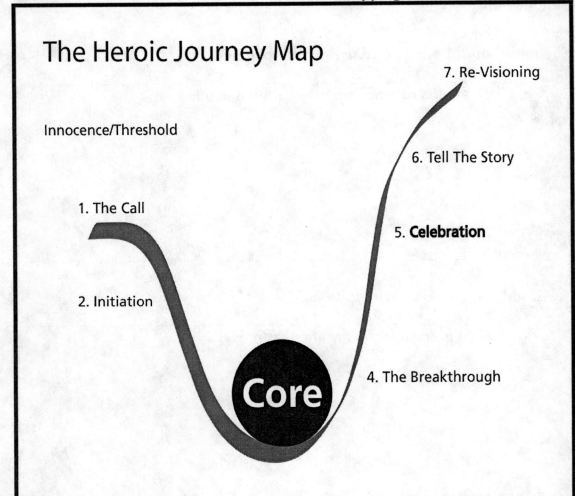

Innocence/Threshold

1. The Call

2. Initiation

Core

4. The Breakthrough

5. **Celebration**

6. Tell The Story

7. Re-Visioning

Stepping into a new way of being demands a celebration of what you have achieved so far.

How will you reward yourself for your efforts to date?

How will you reward those around you that have supported you to date?

What "ah hah!" moments have you experienced?

Over the course of the next couple of weeks, notice your places of inspiration and visit them more often.

Over the course of the next couple of weeks, notice your people of inspiration – those that inspire you to keep going. See if you can spend more time with those individuals.

Celebration and Relationship

To stay within the experience of the Heroic Journey allows you time to reflect upon your life, the journey you have experienced so far and where you might like the journey to change. You have emerged from your journey to this point and it is time to celebrate your achievements. It is easy to see all the things we have yet to accomplish and sometimes hard to remember what has been accomplished to date.

The images you have collected along the way are an important part of your celebration. Those experiences and those images are part of what you now celebrate. Reflect on those people, places and things that are the gifts that sustain you.

My Gifts in Life ...

What are my gifts of purpose?

What are my gifts of vision?

What are my gifts of time?

What are my gifts of relationship?

What are my gifts of prosperity?

What are my gifts of balance?

What are my gifts of creativity?

If you plan on being anything less than you are capable of being, you will probably be unhappy all the days of your life.

Abraham Maslow

Celebration and Recognition

As you list and review what gifts accompany you on your journey, it is important to take the time to stop and recognize and celebrate each gift. How would your life change if you celebrated more and criticized less? For yourself? For your family? For your friends? For your workplace? Joseph Campbell tells us that the birth of personal myth in the imagination of the individual is the seed of rebirth of the greater myth in the imagination of a culture. What would shift for you if you recognize that your imagination is a living symbol for others?

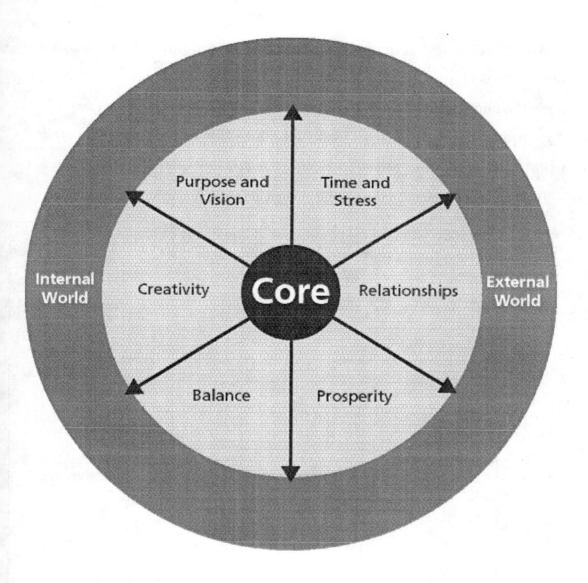

Photocopy the previous pages and place the names of your gifts in each section. Post your Gifts somewhere that you see them every day. A small reminder that regardless of what may go wrong in life, there are many things that go right every day.

Find an image that best represents your gifts – or a multiple board of images that contains all the bounty you possess. Joseph Campbell called this 'bringing home the boon' – the gifts of understanding you have received as a result of your journey. These images feed your core – the deepest part of you that is central to everything you say and do. Your journey is continuous – the destination is to be completely comfortable in your own skin.

What do you feel that your core image or set of images means? Is there a theme that you are beginning to notice?

If this collection of core images could speak, what would they say to you?

What is your gut reaction to what you have noticed?

What colors predominate in your collection? Is there a special relationship for you to color?

Have these core images ever surfaced before for you? Again, is there a potential theme? A recurring one? A call from the past?

What does your core image tell you about your purpose and vision?

What does your core image tell you about your relationship with time?

What does your core image tell you about your relationships?

What does your core image tell you about prosperity?

What does your core image tell you about balance?

What does your core image tell you about your creativity?

Only a life lived in a certain spirit is worthwhile. It is a remarkable fact that a life lived entirely from the ego usually strikes not only the person himself; but observers also, as being dull.

C.G. Jung

Checking In:

How do you feel right now? Are you comfortable with these questions and your responses?

Is there a pattern in your responses? Is there a Celebration necessary with a person or situation you have realized but not acted upon?

Practice Your Power to Choose

For those people who are represented in your core images, it is time to pay a visit. If you cannot meet with them personally, then consider a letter (handwritten and sent through the mail – not email!).

If you can meet with those people who are a gift in your life, set a time and tell that person what they mean to you, how they have helped you, and how important they are to you.

If the person represented is no longer living, write a letter to them expressing your gratitude. You can then burn the letter as an offering or tie it to a balloon and set it free on the wind.

For those situations or things represented in your core images, sit quietly and reflect on the gift given to you.

Choose to celebrate your gifts. Do it deliberately. Do it often.

A hundred times every day I remind myself that my inner and outer life depends on the labors of other men, living or dead, and that I must exert myself in order to give in the measure as I have received and am still receiving.

Albert Einstein

Celebration and Meaning

The value of the Heroic Journey is that it provides a guide that enables a shift in perspective. In order to claim the future, one must also retrieve and claim the past. Holding this tension of the opposites, two seemingly opposing stances, requires a mental shift that can be made and then expanded through the understanding that archetypal psychology promotes. Saying yes to your Call tends to put you on a path that half of you thinks is crazy, but the other half knows that the path will lead to your salvation. "When in doubt about where you are meant to be", a Buddhist saying goes, "look down at your feet."

Part of celebration is to recognize those seekers on a similar journey. Avoid those who preach 'do as I say, not as I do.' Look for those around you who are walking their own path, responding to a call to adventure. And then: seek the stories they tell. A true seeker knows that when you follow a call, you acknowledge an encounter with the divine, the place of deep soul that must be honored. We do not become enlightened by imagining figures of light, Jung once said, but by making the darkness conscious. To tell the tales of these encounters enables others to attempt the journey.

To use story as a container or temenos for this movement or shift in traditional thinking provides a sanctuary. A place of retreat. A place of celebration. A place of rest where you contemplate how you will tell this tale you have lived. That you are still living. And how you wish this story to end.

It is to the telling of this sacred tale we turn next. For as in the Grail Legends, the essential heroic journey results in an act of speech.

The hero, therefore, is the man or woman who has been able to battle past his personal and local historical limitations to the generally valid, normally human forms. Such a one's visions, ideas, and inspirations come pristine from the primary spring of human life and thought. Hence they are eloquent, not of the present, disintegrating society and psyche, but of the unquenched source through which society is reborn.

Joseph Campbell, The Hero with a Thousand Faces

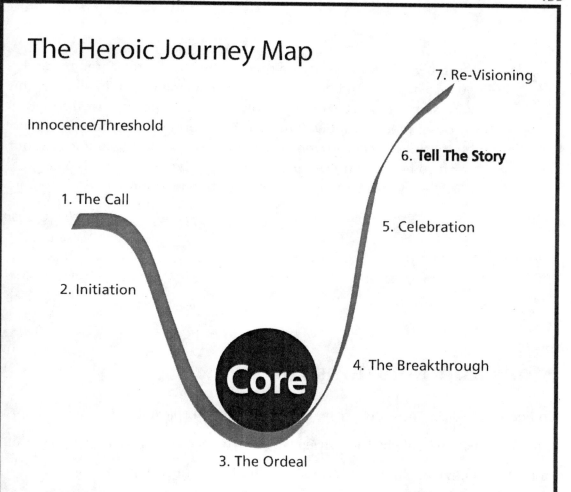

The Heroic Journey Map

7. Re-Visioning

Innocence/Threshold

6. **Tell The Story**

1. The Call

5. Celebration

2. Initiation

Core

4. The Breakthrough

3. The Ordeal

Who are the grandmothers and grandfathers of your tribe?

Collect the tales of the past in order to lay the foundation of your future.

Who are the men and women of the tribe you wish to join?

Collect the tales of these individuals to help you vision your own future.

There is vitality, a life force, a quickening that is translated through you into action---and because there is only one of you in all time, this expression is unique. And if you block it, it will never exist through any other medium and will be lost. The world will not have it. It is not your business to determine how good it is, nor how valuable it is, nor how it compares with other expressions. It is your business to keep it yours clearly and directly, to keep the channel open.

Martha Graham

Story and Relationship

To begin to tell the tales that grow us, takes some preparation. Consciously or unconsciously, we live by the stories we tell. To become aware of the power of story is to realize our power to transform, both for our self and for others.

A primary role of storytelling since the beginning of time is to carry the past into the present. The key to understanding the Jungian or archetypal approach to storytelling or mythmaking, lies in the use of image. Image has the power to pull us out of our limited perspective and see our life from a different lens, a lens that transforms and continues to grow us. Images break through the box we have built around us. Images lead us to our own potential for transformative experience.

Working with images allows you to get beyond your own thinking – image takes you 'out of the box.' Each time you are limited by your own experience – image and metaphor will springboard you into a new way of thinking. As long as you trust your Self to find the path through the unknown. Allow story to carry you through your self-doubt.

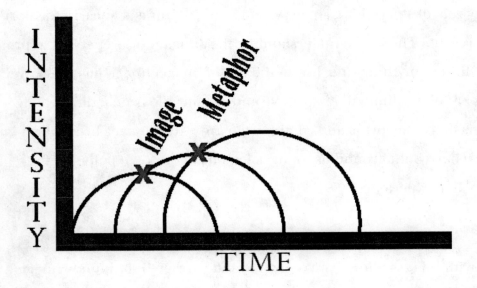

Storytelling then, is probably the most ancient of art forms, the original artistic activity that has propelled the human race since the beginning of time. A good story is polysemous – it suggests a variety of meanings for both teller and listener. In using story as a vehicle forward, we access archetypes of transformation – sources of energy that have been a part of our race from the beginning. To tell the story is to risk exposure – our stories are full of our vulnerabilities, that which makes us human. But, tell the story we must. For in the telling is the healing of the original wound that drove the adventure in the first place. The telling allows the personal experience to become a source of inspiration for others. As Martha Graham said, it is not your business to determine how valuable the story will be. Your task is to tell it.

The whole idea is that you've got to bring out again that which you went to recover, the unrealized, unutilized potential in yourself. The whole point of this journey is the reintroduction of this potential into the world; that is to say, to you living in the world. You are to bring this treasure of understanding back and integrate it into rational life. It goes without saying that this is difficult. Bringing the boon back can be even more difficult than going down into your own depths in the first place.

Joseph Campbell

My Story ... My Life ...

What was the Call?

What was my Initiation?

What was my Ordeal?

What was my Reflection? My Insight? My transformation?

How did I celebrate this transformation? How do I honor this transformation in my story?

Freedom is what you do with what's been done to you.

Jean-Paul Sartre

Story and Recognition

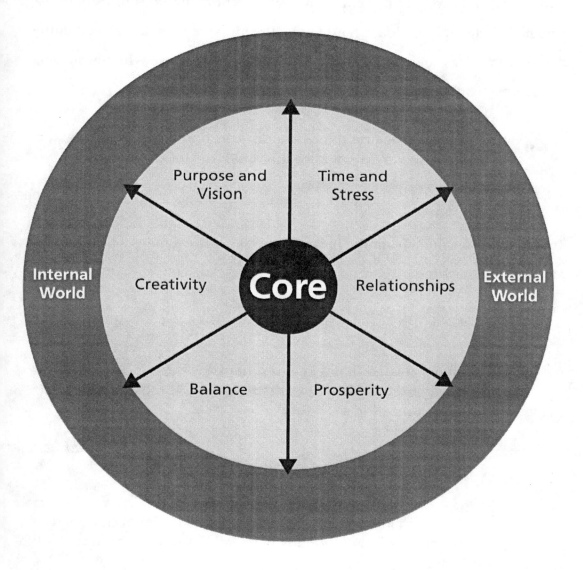

In the last chapter, you were asked to photocopy the previous page and place the names of your gifts in each section and then view them every day.

Now, comes an even greater gift. From each section, tell the stories of those who have fed you in the past. Soul food – the kind we need to keep on going. These are "writes" of passage – a way to immortalize those who have brought us our best teachings.

 It is not because things are difficult that we do not dare; it is because we do not dare that life is difficult.

Seneca

Record those teachers from the past and the specific event by which you received the teaching.

I have argued that a key---perhaps the key---to leadership, as well as the garnering of a following, is the effective communication of a story.

Howard Gardner

When an idea wraps itself around an emotional charge, it becomes all the more powerful, all the more profound, all the more memorable.

Robert McKee

Who taught you about purpose and vision?

Who taught you about the value of time?

Who taught you about relationships?

Who taught you about prosperity?

Who taught you about balance?

Who taught you about creativity?

Stories ... are what animates our 'reasoning process.' Stories .. give us permission to act. Stories ... are photographs of who we aspire to be. Stories ... cause emotional response. Stories ... connect.

Tom Peters

Write the story of each of these events in the third person. Start with:

"Once upon a time ... just yesterday. In a place far, far away ... Just around the corner."

After you have completed each story, mail it to the teacher. In the last chapter, you thanked your teachers for their wisdom and the gifts you have received from them. Now it is time to return the favor.

Life must be lived forwards, but can only be understood backwards.

Soren Kierkegaard

Checking In:

How do you feel right now? Are you comfortable with these questions and your responses?

Is there a pattern in your responses? Is there an untold story with a person or situation you have realized but not acted upon?

Practice Your Power to Choose

 If you always get straight to the point, there may be times when you wonder why you are the only one there.

Annette Simmons

What if consciously cultivating our natural ability to tell stories is the way to tend the life of the soul – feeding it from the inside out. What if consciously cultivating our natural ability for creativity is the way to heal our self, our family, our friends, and our planet?

What if, in order for you to create anything worthwhile in your life, you had to begin right now? From where you are?

The joy of working with image is that when we have no words to describe a situation, drawing the story will give us a start. You don't have to show your drawings to anyone, so please eliminate the voice of judgment! Your body can guide you to a story that wants to be told.

Bring a situation that you have experienced to mind. Sit quietly and allow the story to re-enter your awareness. Using your journal, or a large blank sheet of paper, divide the paper space in half. On one side, write your intention of what you wish to learn from the story - pick a question.

Then close your eyes and take several breaths. Deep breaths. Keep your question in mind. Open your eyes and draw the images that represent your interpretation of the story. What you felt. What you experienced. As the images emerge, sketch them down using whatever tools you choose. Pencil. Pen. Crayon. Charcoal. Paint. Whatever you enjoy.

Now, return to the other side of the page. Start to tell your tale of choice.

"Once upon a time ... just yesterday. In a place far, far away ... Just around the corner."

> **Write down what you know about the images in your drawing. What do they mean to you. What are they saying? Do you have any questions for the images? What do they want you to know?**

Look at your work of art. Is there one image that is trying to get your attention?

What does that image say?

Which image is the main character? Why?

Give this image a name. What do you know about it? Male, female, alive, dead, tall, short, young, old, etc.

Is there a hero? A villan? What other characters are represented in your drawing?

You now have the cast of characters for your story. Tell the remainder of the tale and see if, at the end of your story, you have answered your question from the beginning of this exercise. What is the point of your story? What was the outcome? Every story has a message. What was yours?

Story and Meaning

Then indecision brings its own delays,
And days are lost lamenting over lost days.
Are you in earnest? Seize this very minute;
What you can do, or dream you can do, begin it:
Boldness has genius, power and magic in it.

Loosely translated from Faust, 1835 by John Anster

Victor Frankl survived the horrors of the Nazi concentration camps and turned his experience into the founding of a new field of psychology, logotherapy. Frankl believed that we are not to ask what the events of our lives mean but to take responsibility for creating meaning from the events. His book, Man's Search for Meaning, I find worth reading over and over again.

What if no experience in life is ever wasted? What if each situation, each context, each person played a role in your journey?

What would happen if you cultivated your curiosity? Allowed yourself just to notice what story you are living? Most human beings learn how to talk. To speak, using an authentic voice, requires something more.

In the native teachings of the Medicine Wheel, everything can be viewed from the four directions of the wheel. Using the native wheel of life, try creating your story using different perspectives. Pick a short story about something that happened to you in the last week. Sit for a moment and allow that situation to come to mind. Now use the four directions of the wheel to position yourself. Tell the story from that perspective.

The four directions represent four areas of life: spiritual, mental, emotional and physical. The four colors are used to represent all races: black, red, yellow and white.

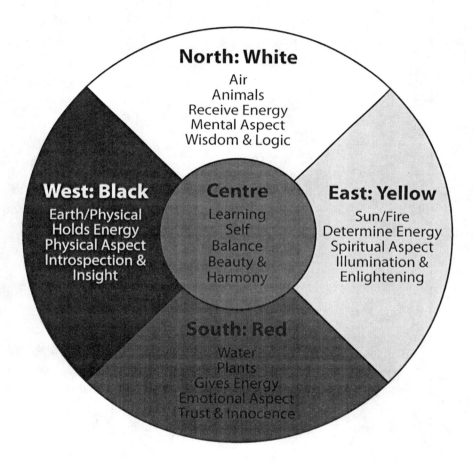

Story Approach from the South (Red). What did you feel? What were the feelings of others? What was trusted? What was betrayed?

Story Approach from the West (Black). Notice the specific sensory details (smell, touch, taste, sound, sight). Notice the physical details and impact of what happened, how it happened, who it happened with and where.

Story Approach from the North (White). Notice what happens from your place of wisdom and understanding. What was your motive in the story? What was the motive of others? What were the causes and effects? What was said? What was heard?

Story Approach from the East (Yellow). Notice what is being taught. What is being learned? What do you now know that you didn't before? If this situation were a dream, what message would it convey?

Your pain is the breaking of the shell that encloses your understanding.

Kahil Gilbran

Merry Mythmaking: A Story Potluck

To keep your commitment to reawaken your ability as a teller, invite some kindred spirits for a potluck. Bring a story to share. Bring a question to be solved.

1.   Decide whether to meet during the week right after work or on a weekend when you might have more time.

2.   You can potluck it, or meet at a local restaurant that has a quiet corner for your tales.

3.   Invite people with various backgrounds and occupations – around eight to ten people gives you variety but keeps the gathering small enough so everyone has a chance to participate.

4.   Write down your questions to be answered on a piece of paper and place them in a sealed envelope before you begin the storytelling.

5.   After each person has told their story – open the envelopes and see how often the question was also answered by the tales.

The Heroic Journey Map

Innocence/Threshold

1. The Call

2. Initiation

Core

3. The Ordeal

4. The Breakthrough

5. Celebration

6. Tell The Story

7. **Re-Visioning**

So ... what comes next?

Rest? Relaxation?

How about another Journey?

> Powering the great ongoing changes of our time is the rise of human creativity as the defining force of economic life. Creativity has come to be valued---and systems have evolved to encourage and harness it---because new technologies, and new industries, new wealth and all other good economic things flow from it. And as a result, our lives and society have begun to resonate with a creative ethos.

Richard Florida

Re-Visioning and Relationship

Albert Einstein was fond of saying that the thinking that created a problem cannot be the thinking that gets you out. The Heroic Journey is an excellent model by which to work but you cannot remain inside the frame. To make progress, we need to re-vision the model and re-member the old version into a modern form. The use of the Heroic Journey as a tool for personal transformation can act as a mirror to a healthy corporate psyche. For our organizations also need to transform.

The future belongs to those who use their hearts as well as their heads – both personally and professionally. A corporate culture is a living mythology so the art of storytelling becomes a foundational tool for any knowledge worker, especially those who aspire to leadership.

In Built to Last, authors Jim Collins and Jerry Porras found that the great companies ask the questions "What do we stand for and why do we exist?" Those same questions have been the focus of this workbook because organizations are made up of people, individuals who search the same questions and seek meaning in the answer.

To set an emergent strategy that allows your story to develop, is necessary for the individual and then the organization. People come first for it is in the individual journey that the corporate culture or even society is shifted. Gandhi stated that we are to be the change we wish to see. So, the journey begins with each one of us.

Strategy is a wonderful tool but by itself is all but useless. Strategy needs tactics – execution – that drive ideas into action. So in order to re-vision yourself, you need both strategy and tactics. Ideas and action.

From your personal strategic plan you outlined in the Call section, how has your strategy changed?

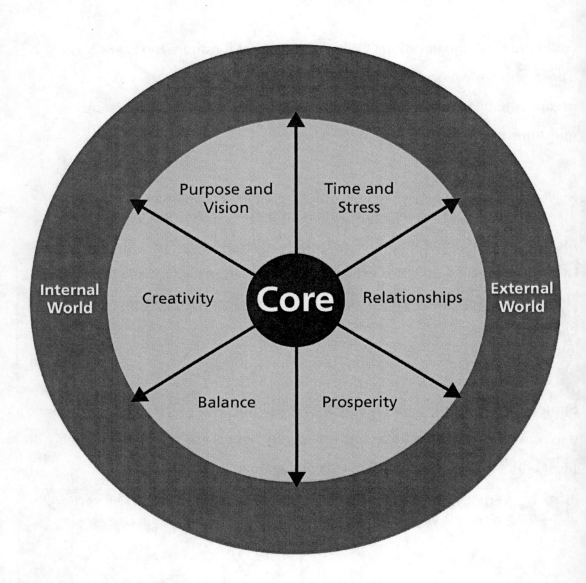

 Live as if you were to die tomorrow. Learn as if you were to live forever.

Gandhi

Schedule some empty time. Put it in your diary, daytimer, your corporate time, your PDA, your crackberry – whatever you use to keep track of where you are and what you are doing. Make it a regular occurrence – once a week, once a month, and if you are very, very lucky – once a day. Call it something important so that others will not attempt to use this space. Keep this time empty.

Re-Visioning My Story ... My Life ...

What is my relationship with my purpose and vision?

What is my relationship with time and stress?

How is my relationship with my self? With others?

What is my relationship with prosperity?

How is my relationship in balance with everything around me?

What is my relationship to my creative source?

We value narrative because the pattern is in our brain. Our brains are patterned for storytelling.

Doris Lessing

Re-Visioning and Recognition

How do I recognize my purpose and my vision?

How do I recognize my use of time? How do I recognize stress? What if the passage of time helps us know what matters most and that, the not knowing causes stress?

How do I recognize my self? My worth. My value. How do I recognize others?

How do I recognize prosperity? How will I know when I have enough?

How do I recognize balance?

How will I know when I am most creative? How will I recognize creativity in others?

Checking In:

How do you feel right now? Are you comfortable with these questions and your responses?

Is there a pattern in your responses? Is there a re-visioning necessary with a person or situation you have realized but not acted upon?

Re-Visioning and Meaning

How do I define meaning in my purpose and my vision? Am I now living my purpose? My vision? Is there anything I need to change or cultivate?

What does time mean to me? What would it mean to have more time? Less time? Enough time? How does this impact my experience of stress?

How do my relationships define meaning for me? What does my relationship with others mean to them?

What does prosperity mean? What does it teach me?

**If my life is in balance, does it add to my experience of meaning?
How so?**

What does creativity mean? To me? To those I love?

We know from the work of C.G. Jung, Joseph Campbell and others that our unconscious mind speaks in images and metaphors. In using this workbook, you have made some of that potential conscious. The more you work with your ability to vision, the more your innate creativity will flourish and continue to feed you. What you vision on the inside will eventually manifest on the outside. If you continue to feed your creative spark, the process will take your ideas into action. You can repeat this process as many times as you wish. Or now do it with your loved ones, family and friends. You can repeat this process at work. Is there a collective vision that needs telling?

So we have come to the end of this journey only to find we are at the threshold of another one. To open the mind to the power of story as an archetypal force is to allow the power of the mythic imagination to break through. Perhaps the meaning we seek is contained in our ability to tell the story ... for ourselves, for each other and for our race.

What would happen if you lived your life as a work of art?

Michael Ray and Rochelle Myer

The canvas is again blank. Remember, you are the hero of your own journey. What is your next adventure?

Blessings for the Journey.

May we all find our way home

ISBN 142511561-6

9 781425 115616